A Tough Problem

by Barbara A. Donovan
illustrated by Kate Hosford

Harcourt
SCHOOL PUBLISHERS

Printed in Mexico

ISBN 10: 0-15-350290-8
ISBN 13: 978-0-15-350290-3

Ordering Options
ISBN 10: 0-15-349940-0 (Grade 5 ELL Collection)
ISBN 13: 978-0-15-349940-1 (Grade 5 ELL Collection)
ISBN 10: 0-15-357327-9 (package of 5)
ISBN 13: 978-0-15-357327-9 (package of 5)

2 3 4 5 6 7 8 9 10   126   12 11 10 09 08 07

Jason liked to take apart old lamps, toasters, and other gadgets. Jason's dad helped Jason and made sure he was careful. Jason wanted to see how these gadgets worked. He put things back the way they were most of the time. Sometimes he could not stop himself. He had to make some changes. He was an inventor, after all.

One morning, Jason's dad burned his fingers taking toast out of the toaster. Jason decided to find a solution to this problem. Jason's dad unplugged the toaster for Jason after it cooled down. Then Jason worked on the device that popped the toast up to the top of the toaster.

Jason realized that the toast did not pop up high enough. The bread only stuck out of the slot the tiniest bit. The bread needed to pop up higher so that people wouldn't burn their fingers when they grabbed it. Jason thought about some solutions to the problem.

Then Jason had an idea. What if he could make the toast pop out of the toaster and fall onto his plate? Everyone could use that kind of toaster. No one's fingers would get burned.

Jason thought the toast should pop up about six inches above the toaster. Then the bread would fall back on a plate beside the toaster. Jason made another change to the toaster. His dad plugged in the toaster. Then Jason put in some bread and waited for it to pop up. Pop! The toast flew straight up into the air. Jason tried to catch the flying toast. His toaster needed more work.

Jason made more changes to the toaster with his dad's help. Sometimes the toast flew up to the ceiling. Sometimes the toast popped up only a few inches. Sometimes it flew about a foot into the air. Jason had to move his plate to catch the toast. This idea was not working yet.

Jason needed a break. He grabbed his baseball glove and a ball. He went next door to his friend Darnell's house. Jason and Darnell started to walk to the park. There they would practice hitting and catching some balls. Jason told his friend about his invention on the way to the park.

The boys agreed to take turns hitting ten balls for each other to catch. Jason batted first. He hit the ball for Darnell to catch. Then they traded places. Darnell hit the first ball high in the air. Jason followed the curve of the ball through the air. He predicted where the ball would land. He stood in that place with his glove wide open in front of him. The ball did not go right or left. It fell just where Jason thought it would. Plop! The ball fell gently into his glove.

Catching that high ball gave Jason an idea. He might be able to make the toast pop out in a high curve like the baseball. Then he could set a plate at a certain spot on the kitchen counter. The toast would fall onto the plate just like the ball fell into his glove. Jason had put several ideas together to come up with a new idea. He was excited about his idea.

At home, Jason asked his dad to unplug the toaster. Then Jason took the toaster apart and looked inside. His dad was nearby in case Jason needed help. Jason planned to change the angle of the part of the toaster that held the bread. The tilted toast would then pop out at an angle. The toast would go high into the air. Then the toast would curve and land on a plate beside the toaster.

Jason worked on the toaster for the rest of the afternoon. He could not find any way to change the angle of the part that held the toast. The slots on top of the toaster were too narrow. If he changed the angle inside, the toast would not pop out of the slots. Jason was getting frustrated.

Slowly, Jason put the toaster back together again. His mind stayed busy with the problem. He put the toaster down on the kitchen table. At first, he did not notice that the toaster wasn't flat on the table. One side rested on a book. Jason was about to return the toaster to the counter. Suddenly, he noticed the toaster was sitting at an angle.

"Of course!" he thought. "I cannot change the angle of the parts that hold the toast. I *can* change the angle of the toaster!"

Jason further experimented with the toaster. He used a board, a book, a box, and other things to change the height of one side of the toaster. He adjusted the device that popped the toast out of the slots. Jason figured out how high the side of the toaster had to be. He also figured out how tight the spring that popped the toast out of the toaster had to be. Everything had to be just right for the toast to pop out of the toaster at the perfect angle and the perfect height.

Finally, Jason stuck two small wooden blocks to the bottom of one side of the toaster. The toaster sat at an angle. Dad plugged the toaster into the wall. By this time, Jason's mom was making a salad for dinner. She was glad that Jason was finished with the toaster. She wanted some toasted bread cubes for the salad. Jason was thrilled. Now he wouldn't have to wait until morning to try his invention.

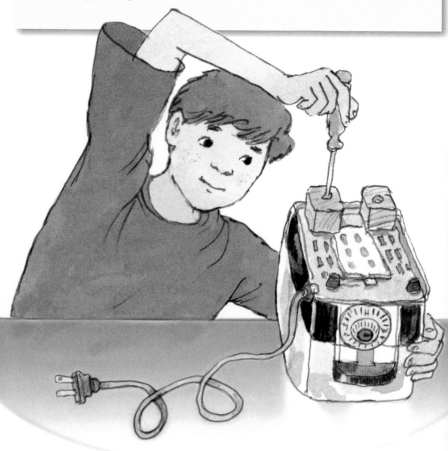

Mom noticed that the toaster now sat at an angle. She was curious about Jason's latest invention. She watched him carefully. Jason took two pieces of bread and put them in the toaster. Then he placed a plate about a foot from the toaster. Jason looked from one parent to the other. "Let's give this a try!" he said.

Jason pressed down the handle. The bread went inside the toaster. Soon the toast flew out of the toaster. The toast flew about a foot into the air. Then it fell gently onto the plate Jason had put there. Mom, Dad, and Jason all clapped and shouted. The family tried the invention again and again. Each time, the toast fell onto the plate just as Jason had planned.

Jason's invention was a success. Jason's dad made a suggestion. Jason should try to get his invention on the game show *Invention Convention*. Many important people watched the show. They wanted new ideas for their businesses. The family believed that Jason's invention was a winner.

Jason liked the game show idea. He began washing the dishes. He thought about how he would present his toaster on the show. Then he looked down at the sink filled with suds and dirty dishes.

"Next on my list is an invention that washes pans and dirty dishes in the sink," he thought. "I wonder how I could make that work." The corners of Jason's mouth lifted. He washed dishes and thought about this interesting new problem.

Scaffolded Language Development

USING PREFIXES Point out the word *unplugged* on page 4 of the text. Write the word on the board and indicate the prefix *un-*. Remind students that a prefix is a word part that is added to the beginning of a word to change its meaning. When the prefix *un-* was added to the word *plugged*, the meaning was changed to "the opposite of *plugged*." Demonstrate plugging and unplugging something in the classroom. Have students identify the prefix in each of the following words and tell how the meaning of the word changed when the prefix was added.

nonfiction	unable	displace
impossible	disagree	improbable
redo	autobiography	untie
nonsense	replay	disappear

Language Arts

Poetry of Invention Have students write a poem from Jason's perspective describing how it feels to see that his invention was successful.

School-Home Connection

Useful Home Appliances Have students go through their house and make a list of all the appliances they use on a normal night. For each of those items, have them discuss with family members what they might have to do or use instead if these appliances had not been invented.

Word Count: 1,184